Target
Get back on track

GRADE 3

AQA GCSE (9–1)
English Language
Writing

Julie Hughes

D1422035

Pearson

Contents

① Gathering ideas for creative writing

This unit will help you to come up with ideas for a narrative or descriptive writing task. The skills you will build are to:

- use an image to find ideas for descriptive writing
- gather ideas for a story structure
- add the ingredients of a good story.

In Paper 1 of the exam, you will be asked to tackle a narrative or descriptive writing task like the ones below. This unit will help you to plan your response.

Exam-style question

You are going to enter a creative writing competition. Your entry will be judged by a panel of people of your own age.

Either: Write a description suggested by this picture.

Or: Write a story about a celebration.

(40 marks)

The three key questions in the **skills boosts** will help you to gather ideas for your creative writing task.

| ① How do I use a picture to gather ideas? | ② How do I gather story ideas? | ③ How do I use the ingredients of a good story? |

Look at three students' story plans on page 2. They were written in response to one of the tasks above.

Write a story about a celebration.

Plan A
- Wake up on my birthday
- No presents on my bed
- No one downstairs
- Feel sad, sit and cry
- Friends rush in shouting 'surprise'
- Go out for celebration and feel really happy

Plan B
- Won lottery
- Spent days buying stuff and celebrating
- Bought mum a house
- Got abuse on social media
- Best friend avoids me
- Start feeling very lonely
- Meet new friend who doesn't know about money

Plan C
- Score winning goal for first team
- Get selected for local league side
- Celebrate with friends who were in crowd
- Play first game for local league side
- Get into bad tackle with other player who is a friend
- Other player has broken leg from tackle
- Get sent off and lose place in team
- Go out and see rest of team celebrating
- Friend won't speak to me
- Spend all my time practising
- Get selected for premier league side
- Score winning goal in cup final
- Celebrate with team
- Friend who broke leg is there but don't speak to him

(1) All of these plans could be improved. Match ✐ the comments with the plans.

Plan A	too many events mean nothing will be developed with interesting details
Plan B	no real ending to story
Plan C	story is dull and a bit predictable: no excitement for reader

(2) (a) Choose one of the plans and write ✐ **two or three** sentences about how it could be improved.

Plan A ☐ Plan B ☐ Plan C ☐

Improvements: ....

....

....

....

(b) This task will be judged by people of your own age. Which plan is **most suitable** for the audience? Explain ✐ your choice.

....

....

....

1 How do I use a picture to gather ideas?

One way to gather ideas for planning a descriptive writing task response is to ask 'who', 'what' and 'where' questions about the picture.

1 Look at the picture in the exam-style question.
A student has started to answer the 'who', 'what' and 'where' questions.
Add some of your own ideas.

? **Who** is there or who might be there? What are they thinking or feeling?

- juggler in bright green suit, might be his first time – looks like he is concentrating hard – might feel ....
....

- young people watching are smiling – they might feel ....
....

? **Where** was the picture taken? Think about the setting. What can you see in the background? What might be hidden?

- busy market area – bars/cafes – people sitting outside
- some people in background are
....
....

? **What** main event is suggested by the picture?

- entertainer trying to break into show business
- spends all day outside a market practising
....
....
....

? **What** might have happened before or after the picture was taken?

- juggler might have worked all day before anybody was interested
- next he might
....
....

2 Imagine yourself in the picture and then use your senses. Think about what you can see, hear, smell, taste and feel. The student has started to do this in the plan below. Add **at least one** more idea to each of theirs.

see ....
....

hear buses in the distance, quiet chatter from the cafes, ...
....

smell diesel fumes from the street, ...
....

taste ....
....

feel sunlight on my face, cobbles under my feet, ...
....

3 Now think about the audience. This will be read by people of your own age. Are any of your ideas unsuitable for that age group? Draw a line through any that are unsuitable.

② How do I gather story ideas?

One way to gather ideas is to use thought association. This means identifying the key word or idea in the title and writing down everything it makes you think about. You can then choose the most exciting or interesting ideas and fit them into a story structure.

① Look at these ideas that a student has thought of related to the idea of 'celebration'. Add
two or three more of your own ideas.

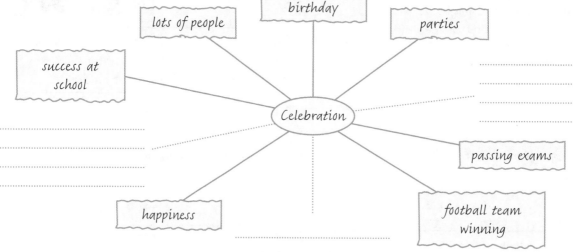

When you have gathered some general ideas, you can think about them in more detail. It helps if you first think about the basic structure of your story.

Beginning – character and setting	**Middle – the event or problem**	**End – the problem is resolved**
Introduces the characters, their situation and the setting.	A problem or crisis happens and needs to be faced by the characters.	The characters deal with the problem. The story can end on a happy or a sad note.

For example, this is how one student has used an idea about celebration. Notice how extra story detail has been added to each stage.

I go to a football match with my dad and my sister Lucy.	*I get lost in crowd.*	*I am found by team's captain.*
The team win on penalties. We all rush on to the pitch to celebrate.	*Very frightened. Push through crowd trying to find Dad and Lucy. Announcement made on tannoy.*	*He takes me to my dad. Then we all get to go and celebrate with team.*

② It is a good idea to stick to one main event so that you can describe it in detail. Use another of the ideas from the spidergram in question ① and fit it into the story structure.

Beginning	Middle	End

3 How do I use the ingredients of a good story?

When you have planned your story structure, it is a good idea to think about whether you have used the ingredients for a good story. These include:
• an engaging plot • interesting characters • some mystery or suspense • a satisfying ending.

Look at this student's plan for a story about a celebration.

Beginning

Woke up on birthday. Had party with friends. Parents gave me new bike. All my friends were jealous. Went out with friends on bike and beat them all. Joined cycling club and raced every weekend. Stopped seeing friends. Entered big national race. Practised every day.

Middle

Race day comes. Wake up nervous. Have big breakfast and drive to race. Big shock on start line. Next to me is best friend. Best friend falls off bike during race. I race past him.

End

I win the race and get my medal. There is no one to celebrate with as all friends are at hospital with my best friend. I celebrate on my own.

1 This student has included too much action and readers might find it boring. Draw a line 🖉 through any action you think is not necessary.

2 The best stories have some mystery or suspense.

a Which of the following ideas would add the most mystery or suspense to the story? Tick ✓ it.

☐ The narrator could find out after he has won that his best friend was in the race.

☐ The best friend could be injured in a crash with the narrator.

b Add 🖉 your own ideas to the plan above to achieve mystery or suspense.

3 Readers like to take sides in a story. It is a good idea to create a hero and a villain.

a Outline 🖉 how a character from the plan above could be made into a hero.

....

....

....

....

....

b Briefly explain 🖉 who could be the villain and how readers could be made to dislike him/her.

....

....

4 Readers like an ending where the hero wins and the villain is punished. Use your ideas for question 3 about characters to note 🖉 down some details to make it either a sad or a happy ending.

....

....

....

Sample response

To plan a successful answer to a narrative writing task, you need to:

- think carefully about the key ideas in the task
- use a three-part story structure
- think about creating heroes and villains, mystery and suspense and a developed ending.

To plan an effective descriptive writing answer, you should:

- ask 'who', 'what' and 'where' questions about the picture
- imagine yourself in the picture and use your senses.

Now look again at this exam-style writing task, which you saw at the start of the unit.

Exam-style question

Write a story about a celebration.

Look at one student's plan for the narrative writing task.

1. How could this plan be improved? Add 🖉 your ideas about heroes/villains and another detail that would add even more mystery or suspense to the story.

2. How could the story end? Think about whether to add a happy or a sad ending. Note 🖉 your ideas in the plan.

> _Beginning_
> Home with friends on winter's night. Celebrating end of exams. Parents away. House is miles from anywhere.
>
>
> _Middle_
> Stranger comes to door. Hands over a parcel. Parcel has 'do not open' written on front. Best friend laughs – says we should open it.
>
>
> _End_

Your turn!

You are now going to **plan** your response to this exam-style task.

Exam-style question

You are going to enter a creative writing competition. Your entry will be judged by a panel of people of your own age.

Either: Write a description suggested by this picture.

① Imagine you are the juggler in the picture. Write 🖉 your ideas for a descriptive writing answer in the spaces below.

> ❓ **Who** can you see? What are they doing? What do you think about them?

> ❓ **Who** are you and what are you doing there?

> ❓ **What** happened before this picture was taken?

> ❓ **What** happened after this picture was taken?

> ❓ **What** can you smell?

> ❓ **Where** are you and why are you there?

> ❓ **What** can you hear?

> ❓ **What** can you feel?

Review your skills

Check up

Review your response to the exam-style question on page 7. Tick ✓ the column to show how well you think you have done each of the following.

	Not quite ✓	Nearly there ✓	Got it! ✓
used a picture to gather ideas	☐	☐	☐
gathered story ideas	☐	☐	☐
used the ingredients of a good story	☐	☐	☐

Look back over all of your work in this unit. Note ✐ down the **three** most important ingredients of a good story.

1. ....

2. ....

3. ....

Need more practice?

Plan your response to the exam-style question below.

Exam-style question

You are going to enter a creative writing competition.

Your entry will be judged by people older than you.

Either: Write a description suggested by this picture.

Or: Write about losing something important.

(40 marks)

How confident do you feel about each of these **skills?** Colour ✐ in the bars.

① How do I use a picture to gather ideas?
☐ ☐ ☐ ☐

② How do I gather story ideas?
☐ ☐ ☐ ☐

③ How do I use the ingredients of a good story?
☐ ☐ ☐ ☐

② Gathering ideas – writing to present a viewpoint

This unit will help you to gather ideas when writing to present a viewpoint. The skills you will build are to:

- establish your point of view
- come up with ideas that express your point of view
- add interesting detail to develop your key ideas.

In the exam, you will be asked to tackle writing tasks like the one below. This unit will prepare you to write your own response to this question.

Exam-style question

'The internet, far from being the greatest invention of the 20th century, is a dangerous and extremely harmful tool.'

Write the text for a speech in which you explain your point of view on this statement.

(40 marks)

The three key questions in the **skills boosts** will help you to gather ideas for when you are writing to present a viewpoint.

| ① How do I decide on my point of view? | ② How do I choose the best ideas? | ③ How do I develop my ideas with interesting detail? |

Exam-style question

'The internet, far from being the greatest invention of the 20th century, is a dangerous and extremely harmful tool.'

Write the text for a speech in which you explain your point of view on this statement.

(40 marks)

Look at how one student has planned for this task.

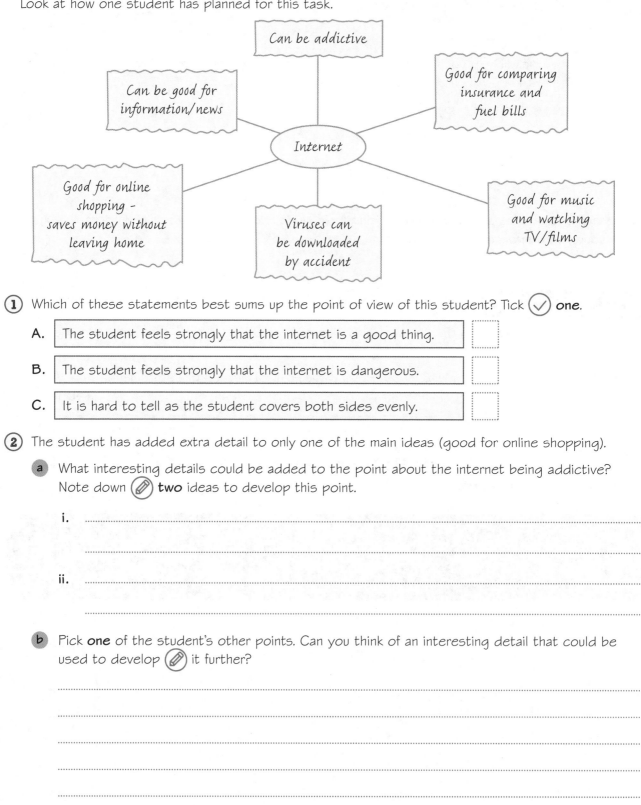

Can be addictive

Can be good for information/news

Good for comparing insurance and fuel bills

Internet

Good for online shopping – saves money without leaving home

Viruses can be downloaded by accident

Good for music and watching TV/films

(1) Which of these statements best sums up the point of view of this student? Tick ✓ **one**.

A.	The student feels strongly that the internet is a good thing.	
B.	The student feels strongly that the internet is dangerous.	
C.	It is hard to tell as the student covers both sides evenly.	

(2) The student has added extra detail to only one of the main ideas (good for online shopping).

a What interesting details could be added to the point about the internet being addictive? Note down 🖉 **two** ideas to develop this point.

i. ....

....

ii. ....

....

b Pick **one** of the student's other points. Can you think of an interesting detail that could be used to develop 🖉 it further?

....

....

....

....

....

How do I decide on my point of view?

Before you begin to gather ideas, you need to decide what point of view you are going to take. To do this, you should first read the question carefully.

Look at how one student has underlined key words in the question and made notes.

> topic is mobile phones

> how annoying it is when people talk loudly on them

xam-style question

'<u>Mobile phones</u> are <u>irritating</u> to <u>those around you</u> when <u>used in public</u>.
They should <u>be banned from all restaurants, cafes and bars</u>.'

Write the <u>text for a speech</u> in which you explain your point of view on this statement.

(40 marks)

> need to agree or disagree with this

> needs to be a speech so need some strong ideas

(1) Now read the question from page 9 again carefully. Underline (A) key words and make notes (✏) in the space around the question about the topic and the format needed.

Exam-style question

'The internet, far from being the greatest invention of the 20th century, is a dangerous and extremely harmful tool.'

Write the text for a speech in which you explain your point of view on this statement.

(40 marks)

To decide which point of view you are going to use, think about which side of the argument you have most ideas about. One way to do this is by thought association. You could write **two lists**, then spend **one minute** thinking of as many points as you can for each one.

(2) Spend **one minute** adding (✏) your own ideas to these lists.

Agree – internet is dangerous	Disagree – internet is a great invention
Can be addictive	Good for keeping in touch
Don't know who you're speaking to online	Useful for research/homework

(3) Now look at your lists. Which one has the most interesting ideas? That is the one you should use as your point of view. Complete (✏) this sentence summing up your point of view.

My point of view about the internet is that it is ....

....

2 How do I choose the best ideas?

When you have decided on your point of view, you will need to choose the best ideas. This involves:

- joining together any of your ideas that are similar
- keeping only those ideas that best support your point of view.

Look at these ideas that a student has come up with for a response to the exam-style question at the start of the unit.

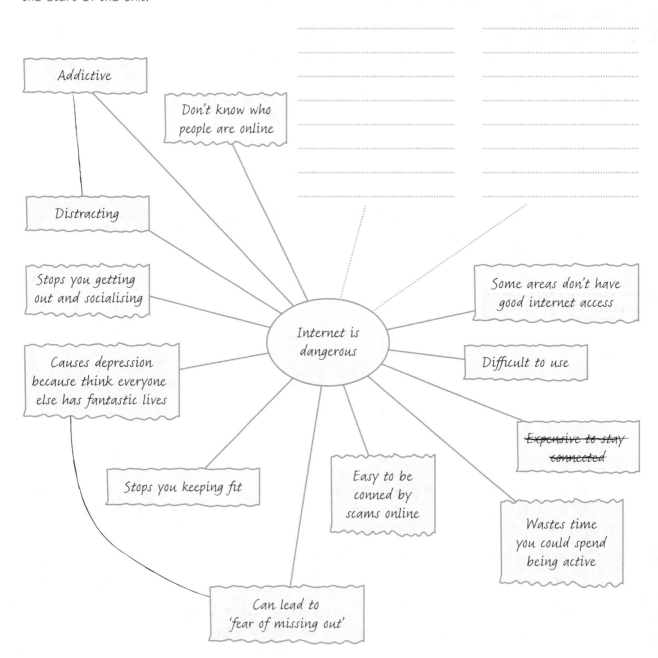

1. The student has already joined some of the ideas together and crossed out one weak idea.

   a. Join 🖉 together any other ideas that are similar.

   b. Cross out 🖉 any you think do not strongly support the point of view.

2. Can you think of any other strong ideas to add to the plan? Try to add 🖉 **two** more. Remember to join them to others if they are similar.

How do I develop my ideas with interesting detail?

When you have gathered your best ideas, you will need to develop them with interesting details. These will make your ideas seem more believable and trustworthy. Details can be:

- facts or statistics
- examples from your own experience.

You can make these up for the exam, but make them believable.

Look at one student's plan for the speech about the internet.

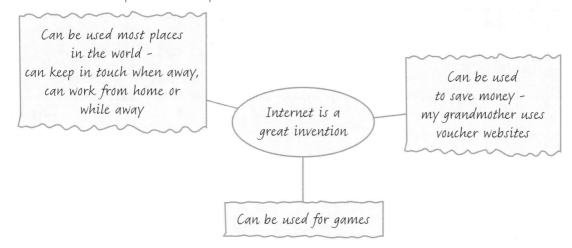

Can be used most places in the world –
can keep in touch when away,
can work from home or
while away

Internet is a
great invention

Can be used
to save money –
my grandmother uses
voucher websites

Can be used for games

1. The idea about games has no detail.

   a. Which of the details below would best support the view that the internet is a great invention? Tick ✓ it.

   b. Which would be unsuitable? Put a cross ✗ by it.

A. My brother plays against friends online.	
B. Doctors say gaming is addictive.	
C. 75% of children's games are educational.	

2. Now look at these ideas from the student's plan on the previous page. Add ✏ detail to each one. Try to use a fact or statistic for one, and a personal experience for the other.

   a. Internet is addictive and distracting

   ....

   ....

   ....

   ....

   b. Causes depression because think others have better lives

   ....

   ....

   ....

   ....

Sample response

When writing to present a viewpoint, you should:

- decide on your point of view by thinking about both sides

- choose your best ideas

- develop your ideas with details like facts, statistics and personal experience.

Now look again at the exam-style writing task from the start of the unit.

Exam-style question

'The internet, far from being the greatest invention of the 20th century, is a dangerous and extremely harmful tool.'

Write the text for a speech in which you explain your point of view on this statement.

(40 marks)

Look at another student's spider diagram plan for this task.

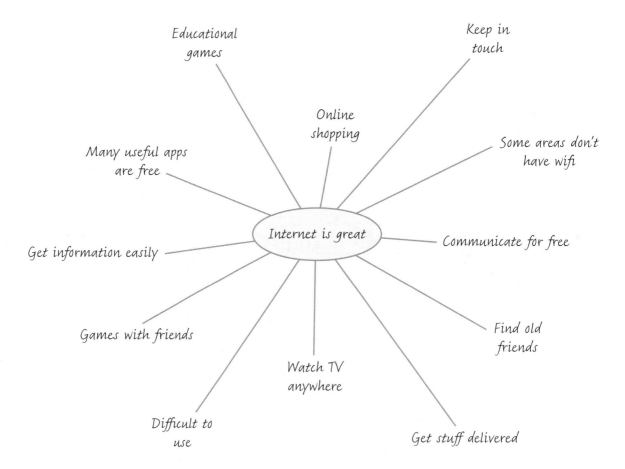

① This plan uses too many ideas.

ⓐ Draw a line 🖉 through any ideas that do not strongly support the point of view.

ⓑ Join 🖉 together any ideas that are similar.

ⓒ Add 🖉 detail to the **three best** ideas.

Your turn!

You are now going to plan your response to this exam-style task.

Exam-style question

'The internet, far from being the greatest invention of the 20th century, is a dangerous and extremely harmful tool.'

Write the text for a speech in which you explain your point of view on this statement.

(40 marks)

(1) Think about what you associate with the word 'internet' for **one minute** to decide your point of view. Use a list or a spider diagram to organise 🖊 your ideas in the space below.

(2) Join 🖊 together similar ideas and cross out ✕ weak ideas.

(3) Now develop 🖊 your **three best** ideas with detail. You can use this table, or draw another spider diagram on paper.

Best ideas	Detail

Review your skills

Check up

Review your response to the exam-style question on page 15. Tick ✓ the column to show how well you think you have done each of the following.

	Not quite ✓	Nearly there ✓	Got it! ✓
decided on my point of view	☐	☐	☐
chosen the best ideas	☐	☐	☐
developed my ideas with interesting detail	☐	☐	☐

Look over all of your work in this unit. Note 🖉 down the **three** most important things to remember when gathering ideas for writing to present a point of view.

1. ....

2. ....

3. ....

Need more practice?

Plan your response to the exam-style question below.

Exam-style question

'Everyone should learn how to cook at school. It is essential for our nation's health that we can all cook basic meals from scratch.'

Write an article in which you explain your point of view on this statement.

(40 marks)

How confident do you feel about each of these **skills?** Colour 🖉 in the bars.

1 How do I decide on my point of view?

2 How do I choose the best ideas?

3 How do I develop my ideas with interesting detail?

(3) Structuring and developing your ideas – creative writing

This unit will help you to structure and develop your ideas for the creative writing task. The skills you will build are to:

- plan an exciting opening and a satisfactory ending to your narrative writing task
- create believable characters
- create an engaging opening to your descriptive writing.

In the exam, you will be asked to tackle writing tasks like the one below. This unit will prepare you to write your own response to this question.

Exam-style question

You are going to enter a creative writing competition.

Your entry will be judged by a panel of people of your own age.

Either: Write a description suggested by this picture.

Or: Write a story about telling a lie.

(40 marks)

The three key questions in the **skills boosts** will help you to structure and develop your creative writing.

1. **How do I begin and end my narrative writing effectively?**
2. **How do I develop interesting characters?**
3. **How do I open my descriptive writing engagingly?**

Look at one student's plan for the narrative writing task above on page 18.

Beginning	Sat in classroom, very bored
	Tom and I are playing with a football
	Teacher keeps telling us to put it away
Middle	I kick football hard and it breaks the window
	Teacher asks who did it
	I say Tom did it
	Tom gets excluded
End	Tom refuses to see me
	Tom spends all his time studying for exams at home
	I mess about at school

(**1**) This student has used a good story structure and kept to two main characters.

   a Think about the **beginning**: which opening would be most effective? Circle (A) your choice.

> (?) A description of the football going through the window

> (?) A description of the boys playing football

> (?) A description of the teacher

   b Write (✏) **one** sentence explaining your choice.

....

....

....

....

(**2**) **a** Think about the **ending**: which ending would be most effective? Circle (A) your choice.

> (?) Tom passes all his exams and goes to university. The narrator never sees him again.

> (?) The narrator meets Tom and apologises. Tom forgives him.

> (?) The narrator ends up unemployed while Tom goes to university and becomes a successful lawyer.

   b Write (✏) **one** sentence explaining your choice.

....

....

....

....

How do I begin and end my narrative writing effectively?

The beginning and end of a piece of narrative writing are very important. Your opening should make readers want to read to the end. Your ending should fully develop the main event. Good stories also show how the main event has affected the characters.

Stories often have exciting first sentences and then use 'flashback' to explain the full story. Look at these openings for the student's narrative plan shown opposite.

Create a mystery – this makes readers want to know what has happened.	Crash! The football sailed from my toe straight out of the window.
Start with conflict or danger – this will create tension from the very beginning.	I know I shouldn't have told the lie. I would regret it for the rest of my life. It was only a small lie at the time, but it caused so much trouble.
Start with action – this grabs the reader's attention as they will want to know more about what is happening.	I froze. The teacher looked up from her marking. Tom and I sat very still and tried to look invisible. My stomach churned with fear.

① **a** Draw lines ✐ to match each technique to a story opening.

b Which opening do you think is the **most** effective? Tick ✓ your choice.

c Write ✐ **one** sentence explaining why.

....

....

② Now think about the ending of the same narrative. One way to make sure your events are fully developed into a satisfying ending is to think about the effect they have had on the characters.

Characters learn a lesson	The narrator messes about at school. Tom works hard with a tutor, goes to university and becomes a successful lawyer. The narrator ends up unemployed and homeless.

a What would the narrator learn from this ending? Note down ✐ your ideas.

....

....

Events set up at the beginning develop and change things for the characters	Tom spends all his time practising football. He gets spotted by a Premier League Club. He becomes famous and tells everybody his success is due to his friend's lie.

b How could this ending change things for the narrator? Note down ✐ your ideas.

....

....

c Stories can also have surprise endings. Write ✐ a surprise ending for the story plan.

....

....

2 How do I develop interesting characters?

To make your narrative writing engaging all the way through, you need to create believable characters. One way to do this is to 'show' what they are like, rather than 'tell'.

Look at these two examples about the character Tom from the story about a lie.

> *A. Tom loved football and played for the school team. Tom was really tall and great at headers.*

> *B. Tom's head nearly hit the classroom ceiling when he headed the ball. The ball sailed towards me over the desks. All the practice with the school team was worth it as everybody turned and clapped.*

In the second example, it is the action that 'shows' rather than 'tells' the reader about Tom. This makes it easier for the reader to picture him and start to like him as a character.

(1) Stories need heroes and villains to make them exciting for a reader. Which of the following uses the 'show not tell' technique to make readers start to hate Tom? Tick ✓ your choice.

> ☐ *A. The ball sailed towards me over the desk. All the practice with the school team paid off as it hit me hard between the eyes. Tom laughed.*

> ☐ *B. The ball sailed towards me over the desk. It hit me between the eyes. He played for the school team and hated me because I was no good at football.*

(2) Try using this 'show not tell' technique to make the narrator into a more believable character.

> *I was thin and small. I had never been any good at football. Nobody ever picked me to be on their team.*

First, decide whether you want the reader to like or hate your narrator. Then think about what action you could use to show the reader, rather than telling. You could think about:

- how the character moves (actions)
- what the character's body language is like
- how other people react to him.

Note down ✐ your ideas below.

Actions ....

....

....

Body language ....

....

....

How other people react ....

....

....

③ How do I open my descriptive writing engagingly?

Your descriptive writing also needs to be exciting from the very first sentence. To do this, think about starting with a description of the setting, a character or the events.

Look at how three students have started their descriptive writing about this picture from the exam-style question on page 17.

| Describing the setting | The sea is spread out like a silver carpet. I can feel the warmth of the sun on my face. I can taste the salty breeze in the air. | ☐ |

| Describing a character | Janet's emerald green eyes shine with excitement. She pushes her long blonde hair out of her face and stares towards the shore. | ☐ |

| Describing the events | We sail silently into the bay. The only sound is the waves lapping gently at the side of the boat. | ☐ |

1. a Which of these openings do you think would be most engaging for a reader? Tick ✓ it.

   b Write ✐ **one** sentence explaining your choice.

   ....

   ....

   ....

2. Now imagine you are on the shore, looking out at the boat in the picture. Using the technique you found most engaging in question ①, write ✐ an engaging opening.

   > Remember to use your senses and think about what you can see, taste, feel, hear and smell.

   ....

   ....

   ....

   ....

   ....

   ....

Sample response

To structure your narrative writing, you need to think about:

- developing your main event into a satisfying ending

- starting with action, mystery or conflict to engage your readers from the very first sentence

- creating believable characters by showing, not telling.

To structure your descriptive writing, you need to think about:

- starting with a description of a character, the setting or the events in the very first sentence.

Look again at the narrative writing task from the exam-style question at the start of the unit.

Exam-style question

Write a story about telling a lie. (40 marks)

1 Now look at one student's plan for this question.

To try to impress a new rich friend, I pretend my father is a rich lawyer who works abroad. She invites me to a very glamorous birthday party. I persuade my parents to buy me a new dress.	I go to the friend's massive house. She says we are going to the party in a limo. The limo turns up and my dad is driving. He is a taxi driver and is driving the limo to make extra money so I can go to uni.	I am too embarrassed to tell the truth. I rush into the house and pretend to be sick. Then I go home.

a Can you think of a more satisfying ending? Write ✎ **one or two** sentences explaining your ideas.

....

....

....

b How could you describe the friend in a way that will show, not tell, that she is rich? Try writing ✎ **one or two** sentences of description.

....

....

....

c Think about which part of the story would make the most engaging opening. Write ✎ the first **one or two** sentences of the story.

....

....

....

Your turn!

You are now going to plan your response to this exam-style task.

Exam-style question

Write a story about telling a lie.   (40 marks)

① Use the following questions to come up with ideas. 🖉   For more help with ideas, see Unit 1.

    ⓐ Who will tell the lie? ....

    ⓑ Why will they tell a lie? ....

    ....

    ⓒ Who are your main characters? ....

    ⓓ What is your main event? ....

    ⓔ What type of ending will you have? ....

    ....

② Use this three-part structure to plan 🖉 your story.

Beginning	Middle	End

③ Now think about the opening of your story. Will you start with mystery, action or conflict? Explain 🖉 your ideas.

....

....

....

④ Look at the ending of your story. Write 🖉 **one or two** sentences explaining how it will satisfy your readers.

....

....

....

⑤ Think about your characters. Use the 'show not tell' technique to write 🖉 **two** sentences that will make one of them believable to your readers.

....

....

....

Review your skills

Check up

Review your response to the exam-style question on page 23. Tick ✓ the column to show how well you think you have done each of the following.

	Not quite ✓	Nearly there ✓	Got it! ✓
begun and ended my writing effectively	☐	☐	☐
developed interesting characters	☐	☐	☐
opened my descriptive writing engagingly	☐	☐	☐

Look over all of your work in this unit. Note ✎ down **three** ways that you can make your writing more engaging to a reader.

1. ....

2. ....

3. ....

Need more practice?

Plan your response to the exam-style question below.

Exam-style question

You are going to enter a creative writing competition.

Your entry will be judged by people who are a similar age to you.

Either: Write a description suggested by this picture.

OR: Write a story about finding something valuable.

(40 marks)

How confident do you feel about each of these **skills?** Colour ✎ in the bars.

1 How do I begin and end my narrative writing effectively?

2 How do I develop interesting characters?

3 How do I open my descriptive writing engagingly?

④ Structuring your ideas – writing to present a point of view

This unit will help you structure your ideas when you are writing to present a viewpoint. The skills you will build are to:

• organise your points into a logical order

• plan an effective opening

• plan an effective conclusion.

In the exam, you will be asked to tackle writing tasks such as the one below. This unit will prepare you to write your own response to this question.

Exam-style question

'Reality TV is full of ageing has-beens and talentless people desperate to be famous. It is an expensive waste of our time.'

Write an article for a broadsheet newspaper in which you explain your point of view on this statement.

(40 marks)

The three key questions in the **skills boosts** will help you to structure your ideas when writing to present a viewpoint.

 How do I organise my ideas into a logical order?

 How do I write an effective introduction?

3 **How do I write an effective conclusion?**

Look at one student's plan for a similar task on page 26.

Exam-style question

'Exams test key skills that are vital in the workplace. They are the best way to test a person's overall abilities.'

Write a speech for an audience of your peers in which you explain your point of view on this statement. **(40 marks)**

Introduction	*Exams are not good for everybody.*
1	*Everybody hates exams at school. Revising means you don't do enough sport and you get unhealthy.*
2	*Exams cause great stress, many young people get ill, families struggle to cope. Use personal experience about own stress at school.*
3	*Exams don't teach you important things like how to manage money or get on with people. Use facts about young people having trouble with money.*
4	*Exams are only good for really clever people. They make more practical students feel a failure. Use examples of friends.*
Conclusion	*Exams don't benefit all young people.*

Look carefully at the plan above. The student has developed the key ideas with interesting details. Now think about the opening, the ending and the order of the points.

(1) Which of these statements about the introduction do you most agree with?
Tick (✓) your choice.

   a   The introduction is interesting and clearly shows the views of the writer.　☐

   b   The introduction is dull and the audience will think the rest of the speech will be boring.　☐

   c   The introduction is effective as it is best to save your good points for the first paragraph.　☐

(2) Which of these statements about the conclusion do you most agree with?
Tick (✓) your choice.

   a   Sum up the writer's feelings and leave a lasting impression.　☐

   b   Just repeat the ideas in the introduction.　☐

(3) Is the sequence of ideas logical and would it make the speech interesting?
Write (✎) **one** sentence explaining your thoughts about the sequence.

....

....

....

....

....

....

How do I organise my ideas into a logical order?

To make your writing to present a viewpoint interesting for a reader, you need to think about where to put your strongest ideas. The sequence of your ideas also needs to be logical.

Look at this exam-style question.

Exam-style question

'Reality TV is full of ageing has-beens and talentless people desperate to be famous. It is an expensive waste of our time.'

Write an article for a broadsheet newspaper in which you explain your point of view on this statement. **(40 marks)**

Now look at one student's plan for this task. The student has sequenced the plan by adding numbers to each idea.

③ 'Airport' and '24 hours in A&E' are important. Show how places work behind the scenes.
Helps people understand important issues.

① Gives families someting to share. Better than living on smartphones. My family enjoys watching 'Celebrity Lifestyles'.

Reality TV

② Gives chances for ordinary people to be on TV. Many entertainers wouldn't get a chance without shows like 'Britains Got Talent'.

④ Not all about celebrities, some shows are educational, like 'Life on Benefits'. Important to learn about other people's lives.

① It is a good idea to start and finish with a strong point.

  a Which **two** are the strongest points in the plan above?

   Renumber ✐ them 1 and 4 in the boxes on the plan.

  b Write ✐ **one** sentence explaining why the point you have chosen as number 1 is the strongest.

   ....

   ....

   ....

② **a** Now look at the two remaining points. Decide which should be the second point and which the third by renumbering ✐ them on the plan.

  b Write ✐ **one** sentence explaining the final order you have used.

   ....

   ....

   ....

2 How do I write an effective introduction?

To engage your reader, you will need to make sure your opening sentence really grabs their attention. To do this, you could use:

- a rhetorical question
- a strong statement that makes your views clear
- a shocking fact or statistic.

① Look at these openings for an exam-style task about reality TV.

A rhetorical question	*Have you ever thought about what it is like to be famous?*	☐
A shocking or interesting fact or statistic	*75% of reality TV shows are about vain, self-obsessed celebrities.*	☐
A strong statement showing your point of view.	*Not all reality TV is about vain, self-obsessed celebrities.*	☐

a Which opening do you think would be best for a speech to your peers? Tick ✓ it.

b Which opening do you think would be best for an article in a broadsheet newspaper? Underline Ⓐ it.

Now look again at this exam-style question you saw earlier in the unit.

Exam-style question

'Exams test key skills that are vital in the workplace. They are the best way to test a person's overall abilities.'

Write a speech for an audience of your peers in which you explain your point of view on this statement. **(40 marks)**

② Write 🖉 **three** possible openings for your response using **three** different techniques:

Rhetorical question: ....

....

Shocking or interesting fact or statistic: ....

....

Strong statement showing your point of view: ....

....

③ Openings that start, 'I am writing to...' are often boring, but there is one type of exam task that needs this style of opening. Tick ✓ the **one** you think should start this way.

A.	A letter applying for a job	☐
B.	A report about school catering	☐
C.	A chapter for a text book	☐

③ How do I write an effective conclusion?

Your final paragraph should leave your reader with a lasting impression.

Look at these ideas for the conclusion to the exam-style task about reality TV.

End with a warning	*Reality TV ruins real life for young people.*	☐
End with a question	*Do you want to end up as a boring couch potato?*	☐
End by asking the audience to take action	*Don't just sit there. Turn off the TV and get outside!*	☐

① **a** Which of these conclusions do you think would be most effective for a speech to young people? Tick ✓ it.

b Which do you think would be most effective for an article in a broadsheet newspaper? Underline Ⓐ it.

Look again at the following exam-style task.

Exam-style question

'Exams test key skills that are vital in the workplace. They are the best way to test a person's overall abilities.'

Write a speech for an audience of your peers in which you explain your point of view on this statement.
(40 marks)

② Use each of the techniques above to write ✏ a conclusion to your response.

A warning: ....

....

....

A question: ....

....

....

Asking the audience to take action: ....

....

....

③ Which of your conclusions do you think would be **most effective**? Write ✏ **one** sentence explaining your choice.

....

....

....

Sample response

To structure your writing to present a viewpoint effectively, you should think about:

- the order of your points, particularly your strongest ideas
- using a strong opening that grabs the attention of your audience
- ending your writing on a strong note that leaves a lasting impression.

Now look at this plan for the writing task about reality TV from the start of the unit.

> *Introduction:* Reality TV is bad
> 1.   *A lot of the celebrities have no talent. They just do reality TV.*
> 2.   *Causes a lot of stress. People try to live like the celebrities.*
> 3.   *Reality TV can be cruel. People are mocked on talent shows.*
> *Conclusion:* *Warn about dangers to young people.*

(1) Rate ✐ the following elements of the student plan out of 5. Explain ✐ your rating in each case.

| The introduction | /5 |

....

....

| The order of the points | /5 |

....

....

| The conclusion | /5 |

....

....

(2) What could this student do to improve the plan? Make ✐ **two** suggestions:

i. ....

....

....

ii. ....

....

....

Your turn!

You are now going to plan your response to this exam-style task.

Exam-style question

'Reality TV is full of ageing has-beens and talentless people desperate to be famous. It is an expensive waste of our time.'

Write an article for a broadsheet newspaper in which you explain your point of view on this statement.   **(40 marks)**

Use the activities below to help you plan your response.

1) a Underline Ⓐ key words in the question so that you are sure of the audience, purpose and format.

   b Make notes ✐ to plan for the audience, purpose and format you have identified.

   ....

   ....

2) a Now use the key words in the question to come up with some ideas ✐. Here are some prompts to help you.

| ? What are the different types of reality TV? Are some better than others, or are they all a waste of time? | ? Why do people watch reality TV? Do they enjoy it, or do they just enjoy watching people suffer? | ? What are my views on reality TV? Are all celebrities talentless, fame-seeking has-beens? |

   ....

   ....

   ....

   ....

   ....

   b Add ✐ details like facts, statistics or personal experiences to your ideas.

   c Draw ✐ a line through any points that are weak or repetitive.

3) Which of your points is the strongest? Number ✐ them in order of importance.

4) Write ✐ an engaging introduction that will grab the attention of your reader.

   ....

   ....

   ....

5) Now plan a conclusion that will leave a lasting impression. ✐

   ....

   ....

   ....

Review your skills

Check up

Review your response to the exam-style question on page 31. Tick ✓ the column to show how well you think you have done each of the following.

	Not quite ✓	Nearly there ✓	Got it! ✓
organised my ideas into a logical order	☐	☐	☐
written an effective introduction	☐	☐	☐
written an effective conclusion	☐	☐	☐

Look over all of your work in this unit. Note 🖉 down **three** things that you should remember to do when structuring your writing to express a point of view.

1. ....

2. ....

3. ....

Need more practice?

Plan your response to the exam-style question below.

Exam-style question

'There's nothing really wrong with eating fast food when you're young. You've got the rest of your life to worry about your health and fitness.'

Write a speech for an audience of your peers explaining your views about this statement.

(40 marks)

How confident do you feel about each of these **skills?** Colour 🖉 in the bars.

1 How do I organise my ideas into a logical order? ☐☐☐☐

2 How do I write an effective introduction? ☐☐☐☐

3 How do I write an effective conclusion? ☐☐☐☐

⑤ Making your meaning clear – sentences

This unit will help you to express your ideas clearly. The skills you will build are to:

- start and end your sentences correctly to make your meaning clear
- join your sentences together to develop your ideas
- use punctuation to make your meaning clear.

In the exams, you will be asked to tackle writing tasks like the ones below. This unit will prepare you to write your own response to one of these questions.

Paper 1

Exam-style question

Describe a time when you made a serious mistake.   (40 marks)

Paper 2

Exam-style question

'Winning is everything. There is no point competing if you don't want to win.'

Write a speech for an audience of young people in which you explain your point of view on this statement.   (40 marks)

The three key questions in the **skills boosts** will help you to make your meaning clear.

1 How do I start and end a sentence?

2 How do I join my ideas into longer sentences?

3 How do I use punctuation correctly?

Now read one student's response to the Paper 1 exam-style writing tasks on page 33.

Paper 1

Exam-style question

Describe a time when you made a serious mistake. (40 marks)

> My mistake was to move to the city from the country, where I grew up
> surrounded by the sounds and smells of nature, with lots of friends and
> family around me. When I left school I moved to the city to a job in a
> large jewellery shop I thought would be exciting but it was just a confusing
> deafening place, I had to leave all my friends behind, I was lonely,
> convinced I would never feel at home.

(1) Read the response carefully and annotate 🖉 the sentences. Think about:

a the length of the sentences (Are they too long to make the meaning clear?)

b whether the punctuation helps to make the meaning clear.

Now read another student's response to the Paper 2 exam-style writing task on page 33.

Paper 2

Exam-style question

'Winning is everything. There is no point competing if you don't want to win.'

Write a speech for an audience of young people in which you explain your point of view
on this statement. (40 marks)

> Do you think winning is important. I think it is very important! It
> teaches people valuable skills like resilience and perseverance! My friend
> barry works at a Fast Food restaurant. The restaurant has a competition
> every month to see who sell's the most burger's. barrys obsessed with
> winning so he works even harder than usual. Without the competition
> barry tells me he would find the job dull repetitive and lacking in
> challenge.

(2) Read the response carefully and annotate 🖉 the sentences. Pay attention to:

a the use of capital letters

b the punctuation at the end of sentences

c the use of apostrophes

d whether any sentences could be joined together to make the meaning clearer.

How do I start and end a sentence?

You must start all your sentences with a capital letter and end them with a full stop, an exclamation mark or a question mark. A common error with sentences is using a comma to join two pieces of information instead of a full stop to separate them.

When you want to give the reader two pieces of information, you can do **two** things.

- Separate them with a **full stop**:

My first mistake was to move to the city. It was a deafening, confusing and very unfamiliar place.

- Join them with a **linking word**:

My first mistake was to move to the city **as** it was a deafening, confusing and very unfamiliar place.

You **cannot** join them with a comma:

~~My first mistake was to move to the city, it was a deafening, confusing and very unfamiliar place.~~

(1) Cross out ✏ the commas in this response and join or separate ✏ the sentences correctly, using a conjunction or a full stop:

I loved my job in the city, I worked in a large fashion store and loved meeting lots of different people. I should never have moved to the country, I had to leave all my friends behind. The countryside was very green and peaceful, it was sometimes too quiet.

Exclamation marks can be used to end a sentence if you want to show excitement or danger.
Be careful: too many exclamation marks can mean they lose their impact.

(2) Add ✏ an exclamation mark to **one** of these sentences to add a sense of excitement.

One of my biggest mistakes in the country was not to listen to warnings about animals. I wanted to make the most of nature so I explored for hours every day. Many of the fields were full of what I thought were cows. I only found out they were bulls when one charged at me. They had all looked friendly from a distance.

(3) The student who wrote the following response has used too many exclamation marks and has also forgotten a question mark and a capital letter. Correct ✏ the mistakes and add ✏ just **one** exclamation mark.

I always want to win even if I am just playing Monopoly with my mates! who doesn't want to win. Those who say winning doesn't matter are just losers! They probably just don't want to try hard at anything! Competition is good for you as you learn something even if you don't come first.

2 How do I join my ideas into longer sentences?

To make your writing more interesting and develop your meaning, you can join simple sentences together to make longer ones. You can do this by using linking words such as 'and', 'or', 'but', 'because', 'although', 'unless', 'if', etc. These each have different effects and help to serve your intention.

You can join simple sentences together to make your meaning clear.

- Use 'but' or 'although' to show that there are two different points of view:

> *Winning is very important to most people* **although** *there are some who think taking part is more important...*

- Use 'and' to join two points, or to add a point:

> *...***and*** I agree with them...*

- Use 'because' or 'as' to explain your point:

> *...***because*** it teaches valuable lessons.*

- Use 'or' to show alternative ideas:

> *Sport can be played to win* **or** *it can simply be played for fun...*

- Use 'so' to show the consequence of your point:

> *...***so*** it's quite easy to take some exercise...*

- Use 'if' or 'unless' to add a condition to your point:

> *...***unless*** you want to end up as a couch potato!*

① ⓐ Look at these simple sentences from one student's response about winning. Join the first sentence to each of the others by choosing one of the linking words to make your meaning clear.

and	or	as	although	but

Taking part in competitions is good for you.		Competing can teach you valuable skills like perseverance and resilience.
		Not everybody thinks winning is important.
		You can just play sport for enjoyment.

ⓑ Now look at these simple sentences from another student's response about losing. Think about the meaning you want to convey. Join the first sentence to each of the others by using one of the linking words.

if	or	so	and	because

We all need to learn what it is like to lose.		Competitive sport is very important.
		We want to appreciate the joy of winning.
		I personally have never won a single race.

3 How do I use punctuation correctly?

You should use punctuation correctly to make your meaning clear or help develop your meaning. Commas can be used to separate information within a sentence.

You can use commas to add extra information in the form of a list.

For example you can add a list of:

adjectives	noun phrases
He was tall, smartly dressed and very good-looking.	My friend won the essay competition at school, the player of the year title at football and the best dressed award at the Summer Prom.

1 Complete ✏ these sentences by listing information using **commas**.

a Add **adjectives**: The weather was ....

....

b Add **noun phrases**: We all need to learn ....

....

You can also add extra information to a sentence by using one of these **pronouns**.

that	who	which
whose	where	when

For example:

The house always looked dark and frightening.	The house, **which** stood on the top of a steep hill, always looked dark and frightening.	Notice how the additional information appears between **commas**.
My brother thinks that winning is the most important thing in the world.	My brother, **who** plays professional football, thinks that winning is the most important thing in the world.	

2 Practise adding ✏ information to these sentences using **pronouns** from the table above.

Remember to place the new information between **commas**.

a My friend told me I was making a big mistake.
My friend, ...

...., told me I was making a big mistake.

b It was at the park that I made my first mistake.
It was at the park, ...

...., that I made my first mistake.

c My first football trophy stands on the mantelpiece.
My first football trophy, ...

...., stands on the mantelpiece.

Sample response

To make the meaning of your sentences clear, you need to think about:

- the way you start and end sentences
- joining simple sentences together to make your writing more interesting
- using commas to add extra detail to your sentences.

Look at the paragraph below from one student's response to this exam-style writing task from page 33.

Exam-style question

Describe a time when you made a serious mistake.

(40 marks)

My big mistake was telling everything to my friend Alice! Alice was the perfect friend. We did everything together. I thought she was the kindest funniest person I had ever met. As we grew up we shared clothes make-up and even our deepest secrets about everything. When I met John at tennis lessons I told Alice how much I liked him. I knew she would want to meet him. I didn't think she would want him for herself!

(1) How could the sentences be improved to develop the writer's meaning? Redraft ✐ the paragraph in the space below, thinking carefully about these ideas:

- Can extra detail be added to any sentence? (Perhaps something about Alice or John?)
- Are both exclamation marks adding meaning?
- Are any commas missing?
- Can any sentences be joined together to form longer sentences that develop the writer's meaning?

....

....

....

....

....

....

....

....

....

....

....

....

....

Your turn!

Choose one of the two exam-style tasks you saw at the beginning of this unit.

Exam-style question

Describe a time when you made a serious mistake. (40 marks)

Exam-style question

'Winning is everything. There is no point competing if you don't want to win.'

Write a speech for an audience of young people in which you explain your point of view on this statement. (40 marks)

You are going to **plan** and **write** the first two paragraphs of your response, focusing on sentence structure and punctuation.

1. Use this space to note down all the different ideas for your response.

2. a. Choose the ideas that you will focus on in your opening two paragraphs. Tick them.

   b. Think about any extra details you could add to the ideas for these two paragraphs. Make a note of them below.

3. Now write the first two paragraphs of your response on paper, thinking carefully about:

   - the way you start and end sentences
   - joining simple sentences together to make your writing more interesting
   - using commas to add detail to your sentences.

Review your skills

Check up

Review your response to the exam-style question on page 39. Tick ⊘ the column to show how well you think you have done each of the following.

	Not quite ⊘	Nearly there ⊘	Got it! ⊘
started and ended a sentence	☐	☐	☐
joined my ideas into longer sentences	☐	☐	☐
used punctuation correctly	☐	☐	☐

Look over all of your work in this unit. Note down ✏ **three** things you can do to improve your sentences.

1. ....

2. ....

3. ....

Need more practice?

You could either:

• add a paragraph to your response to the task you chose on page 39

or:

• tackle the other writing task on page 39.

How confident do you feel about each of these **skills?** Colour ✏ in the bars.

1 How do I start and end a sentence?

2 How do I join my ideas into longer sentences?

3 How do I use punctuation correctly?

⑥ Writing sentences to create impact

This unit will help you write sentences that create impact. The skills you will build are to:

- open your sentences in a variety of interesting ways
- structure your sentences in a variety of interesting ways
- use short minor sentences to create impact.

In the exam, you will be asked to tackle writing tasks like the ones below. This unit will prepare you to write your own response to one of these questions.

Paper 1

Exam-style question

You are going to enter a creative writing competition.

Your entry will be judged by a panel of people of your own age.

Write a story about receiving bad news.   **(40 marks)**

Paper 2

Exam-style question

'Donating money to charity is a waste of time. Not all of the money gets to good causes.'

Write an article for a broadsheet newspaper explaining your point of view on this statement.   **(40 marks)**

The three key questions in the **skills boosts** will help you to write sentences to create impact.

① How do I open my sentences to create impact?

② How do I structure my sentences to create impact?

③ How do I use short sentences to create impact?

Look at extracts from one student's answers to the exam-style tasks above on page 42.

Paper 1

Exam-style question

Write a story about receiving bad news.

> I was driving us home from the party when she told me the bad news. The radio was very loud and Sarah was humming along to a tune she likes. She stopped humming and mumbled something quietly. I didn't hear her at first so she said it again loudly. I turned to stare at her when I finally realised what she was telling me. I took my eyes off the road for too long and crashed the car into a tree.

(1) Which of the following would give this paragraph more impact? Tick ✓ **two.**

A.	Using a variety of different words to open each sentence.	☐
B.	Using a short sentence to create tension about the car crashing.	☐
C.	Starting each sentence with the pronoun 'I'.	☐
D.	Using very long sentences to add lots of detail.	☐

Paper 2

Exam-style question

'Donating money to charity is a waste of time. Not all of the money gets to good causes.'

Write an article for a broadsheet newspaper explaining your point of view on this statement.

(40 marks)

> Some people give money to charity because they feel guilty for having a nice life. Other people give to charity because they have somebody in their family who is ill or needs help. Some people give to many charities because they are lucky enough to have too much money to spend on themselves.

(2) Which statement best describes the sentences in this paragraph? Tick ✓ **one.**

A.	The sentences use a variety of structures to create impact.	☐
B.	The sentences use a variety of openings to create impact.	☐
C.	The paragraph lacks impact as the sentences are all similar in structure.	☐
D.	The sentences are all too short to create impact.	☐

How do I open my sentences to create impact?

Thinking about the first word of a sentence can create impact and make your writing more interesting to read. You can start a sentence with any of these.

Type of word	Examples
A pronoun (a word which stands in the place of a noun) I, you, he, she, it, we, they, my, your, his, her, our, their	I crashed the car when I heard…
A preposition (a word which tells you the position of something or someone) above, behind, between, near, with, on, under	**Between us** blared the radio, which drowned out Sarah's words…
An 'ing' verb (an action word) running, hurrying, waiting, holding	**Raising** money for charity can make people feel…
An adjective (a describing word) slow, quiet, large, huge	**Huge** amounts of money are raised each year…
An adverb (a word that describes a verb) alarmingly, painfully, happily, quickly	**Surprisingly**, over 50% of people never give any money to charity… If you use an adverb at the start of a sentence, remember to put a comma after it.

1 Write 🖉 **five** sentences about giving money to charity. For each one, use a different opening from the table above.

i. ....

....

ii. ....

....

iii. ....

....

iv. ....

....

v. ....

....

2 How do I structure my sentences to create impact?

Structuring your sentences in different ways can change the impact of your ideas.

Read the sentences below in which a student writes about people who donate to charity.

This sentence makes people's **laziness** the most important idea as it is positioned towards the end of the sentence:

> People donate to charity out of guilt because they are too lazy to do anything practical to help others.

This sentence emphasises people's **guilt** as this information comes at the end of the sentence:

> People are too lazy to do anything practical to help others so they donate to charity out of guilt.

(1) Change the structure of this sentence to make **poverty** the most important point.
Write ✐ your new version here.

> The government would have to do more about poverty if we all stopped donating to charity.

....

....

(2) The impact of a sentence can be changed by varying the position of the information within it.
Look at these two versions of a sentence in which a student writes about receiving bad news.

Version 1

> [1] I turned to stare at her [2] when I finally realised what she was telling me [3] and took my eyes off the road for too long.

Version 2

> [2] When I finally realised what she was telling me [1] I turned to stare at her [3] and took my eyes off the road for too long.

a Practise ✐ restructuring the sentence in **two** more ways.

Version 3 ....

....

....

Version 4 ....

....

....

b Which version (including your own) creates the most impact? Write ✐ **one** sentence explaining your choice.

....

....

3 How do I use short sentences to create impact?

Short sentences can be particularly effective when you want to add impact to an argument or tension to a story.

Look at this student's paragraph in response to the Paper 2-style question on page 41 about donating to charity.

> *Many charities rely on donations to provide help to those most in need. It is often only because of charity organisations that children in poorer countries have access to clean water, healthy food and vaccinations. Without these charities, many thousands of children would die each day. Our donations keep them alive.*

Here the final short sentence adds **impact** as it follows several longer sentences.

1. Practise using short sentences by adding 🖉 **two** sentences to the following paragraph. Make **one** of your sentences short, to add impact.

> *It is often only because of charity donations that children in poorer countries have access to clean water, healthy food and vaccinations. Many people feel helping those abroad is wrong as we have children in this country who need help.*

....

....

....

....

....

Now look at how a short sentence can be used to add **tension** to a story.

> *My heart began to race, blood rushed into my ears and my vision went blurry. My stomach was churning and I could feel my legs shaking. As I stared into the gloom I could just see the door beginning to open in the distance. I froze.*

2. Practise using short sentences to add tension by replacing 🖉 the last two sentences above with **two** of your own.

> *My heart began to race, blood rushed into my ears and my vision went blurry. My stomach was churning and I could feel my legs shaking.*

....

....

....

....

....

Sample response

To write sentences that create impact and are interesting to read you need to think about:

- using a variety of words at the start of your sentences
- how you structure your sentences
- using short sentences to create impact or tension.

Now look at this exam-style task which you saw at the beginning of the unit.

Exam-style question

Write a story about receiving bad news.

> It had started as just an ordinary day for me. When the bombshell
> was dropped I was just drumming my fingers on the steering wheel,
> concentrating on the heavy traffic ahead and thinking about what to have
> for dinner. Mumbling quietly under her breath, Sarah gave me the bad
> news. I turned to stare at her when I finally realised what she was telling
> me. The steering wheel slipped from my grasp as dancing stars appeared in
> front of my eyes and blood rushed into my ears. I crashed the car.

1. Read the extract from one student's response above. Try reading it aloud so that you can hear the impact of the sentences. Then annotate 🖉 the paragraph, making notes about the effectiveness of:

   a **the sentence openings**: are they varied and do they create impact?

   b **the sentence structures**: could any sentences be restructured to create more impact?

   c **the final short sentence**: how does it create impact?

2. Can you think of an alternative final sentence? Write 🖉 it below.

....

....

....

....

Your turn!

Choose **one** of the two exam-style tasks you saw at the beginning of this unit.

Paper 1

Exam-style question

You are going to enter a creative writing competition.

Your entry will be judged by a panel of people of your own age.

Write a story about receiving bad news. **(40 marks)**

Paper 2

Exam-style question

'Donating money to charity is a waste of time. Not all of the money gets to good causes.'

Write an article for a broadsheet newspaper explaining your point of view on this statement. **(40 marks)**

You are going to plan and write the first **two** paragraphs of your response. You should focus on writing sentences that create impact.

1) Use the box below to note down some ideas. (Space your notes out so you can add more detail later.)

2) Tick the ideas that you will focus on in your two paragraphs. Make sure you have added enough detail to the ideas you have chosen. Add more if necessary.

3) Now write your **two** paragraphs on paper, thinking carefully about:

- the words you use at the start of your sentences
- the way you structure your sentences
- using short sentences to create impact.

Review your skills

Check up

Review your response to the exam-style question you chose on page 47. Tick ✓ the column to show how well you think you have done each of the following.

	Not quite ✓	Nearly there ✓	Got it! ✓
opened my sentences to create impact	☐	☐	☐
structured my sentences to create impact	☐	☐	☐
used short sentences to create impact	☐	☐	☐

Look over all of your work in this unit. Note down 🖉 **three** ways you can add impact to your sentences.

1. ....

2. ....

3. ....

Need more practice?

You could either:

• add a paragraph to the task you chose on page 47

or:

• tackle the other writing task on page 47.

Remember to focus on creating impact through your choice of sentence structure.

How confident do you feel about each of these **skills?** Colour 🖉 in the bars.

1 How do I open my sentences to create impact?

2 How do I structure my sentences to create impact?

3 How do I use short sentences to create impact?

Use a range of sentence structures for clarity, purpose and effect (AO6)

⑦ Writing paragraphs to create impact

This unit will help you write paragraphs that will create impact and make your meaning clear. The skills you will build are to:

- use clear paragraphs to separate your ideas
- structure and develop your paragraphs to make your meaning clear
- structure your paragraphs to create impact.

In the exam, you will be asked to tackle writing tasks like the ones below. This unit will prepare you to write your own response to one of these questions.

Paper 1

Exam-style question

Your local library is asking people to contribute creative writing for its website.

Write a story about an unexpected visitor. **(40 marks)**

Paper 2

Exam-style question

'Teenagers are far too unfit these days. The only answer is to make them do one hour of physical education every day at school.'

Write an article for a broadsheet newspaper in which you explain your point of view on this statement. **(40 marks)**

The three key questions in the **skills boosts** will help you to write paragraphs to create impact and make your meaning clear.

| ① How do I start paragraphs? | ② How do I structure my paragraphs to make my meaning clear? | ③ How do I structure my paragraphs to create impact? |

Look at the extracts on page 50 from two students' answers to the exam-style tasks above.

Paper 1

Exam-style question

Your local library is asking people to contribute creative writing for its website.

Write a story about an unexpected visitor. (40 marks)

> *Ben jumped up in shock because a loud knock at the door woke him. He crept slowly into the hall and reached for his doorkeys. He wondered who was calling so late on a weeknight.*

(1) Is this paragraph structured so that it creates impact? Write ✐ a sentence explaining your answer.

....

....

....

Paper 2

Exam-style question

'Teenagers are far too unfit these days. The only answer is to make them do one hour of physical education every day at school.'

Write an article for a broadsheet newspaper in which you explain your point of view on this statement. (40 marks)

> *Teenagers spend most of their lives in front of a computer screen. Many teenagers, particularly boys, spend hours playing computer games. Girls spend hours on the internet. This can lead to depression and isolation. Most teenagers do not take the recommended amount of exercise each day. I see young people catch the bus to school even if they live close enough to walk. Most children do not take part in any organised sports. This is increasing teenage obesity.*

(2) This student has two different ideas but they have all been put into one long paragraph. Each new idea or point should have a new paragraph. Mark ✐ where a new idea has been introduced.

(3) What is the topic of each paragraph in the student's response? Complete ✐ the sentences.

   (a) Paragraph 1 is about ....

....

....

....

   (b) Paragraph 2 is about ....

....

....

....

(4) Each paragraph should be developed with evidence. In the student answer above, underline Ⓐ the sentences that contain evidence.

1 How do I start paragraphs?

You need to use paragraphs to organise your points and make it easier for your readers to follow your ideas.

When writing to express your point of view, you should start a new paragraph each time you start a new point. Each paragraph should start with a sentence that clearly introduces the content of the paragraph. This is called a topic sentence. For example:

> <u>Our school makes a big effort to encourage teenagers to take exercise</u>. All students are given time after lunch to take part in organised activities such as football, basketball and gymnastics. The school also has many sports teams that train after school. Even the staff play 5-a-side football, although they are usually beaten!

1) Add a topic sentence to this paragraph from a student's response to the exam-style question on page 50.

....

....

> Most teenagers catch the bus to school, use escalators instead of stairs and rely on their parents for lifts rather than walking anywhere. Behind my house is a school and the road is blocked every day with parents dropping off or collecting children who live less than a mile away. This is increasing teenage obesity.

For creative writing, it is a good idea to start a new paragraph:

- when you move forwards or backwards in time
- when you move to a new setting
- when you introduce a new character, or change to another point of view.

For example:

> Ben settled back in his chair in front of the fire. It had been a long day and all Ben could think about was his aching back, his sore feet and his frozen hands. Finally, he was able to sit down and relax. Sighing happily, Ben closed his eyes for a sleep.
>
> Outside, heavy rain was battering against the windows and wind was howling through the trees. Leaves blew around the garden. The surface of the pond was beginning to freeze over and icicles were starting to form on the roof.

2) Practise writing two different opening sentences to the next paragraph of this story by moving forwards or backwards in time, or by introducing a new character.

i. ....

....

....

ii. ....

....

....

② How do I structure my paragraphs to make my meaning clear?

When writing to express your point of view, it is important to structure your writing clearly to make your meaning clear. One way to do this is to use a Point–Evidence–Explain (P.E.E.) structure:

- A clear **point** should be made in the topic sentence.
- **Evidence** should be used to prove the point. Evidence can be facts, statistics or examples.
- An **explanation** should be given to link the evidence to the point.

① Look at this student's paragraph in response to the exam-style question on page 49.

> Teenage obesity is a big problem in the UK. A recent survey showed that eighty-five percent of teenagers do not take the recommended daily amount of exercise. Instead of playing sports outside, they are spending all their time in front of a computer screen. This inactivity will make the obesity situation a lot worse if we do nothing.

Underline Ⓐ the **point**, the **evidence** and the **explanation** in the above paragraph.

② ⓐ Complete ✍ these P.E.E. paragraphs by adding evidence and an explanation that links your evidence to the point. Try to add interest by including **more than one** piece of evidence.

> Exercise at school does not have to be boring.
>
> ....
>
> ....
>
> ....
>
> ....
>
> ....
>
> Daily exercise has many benefits.
>
> ....
>
> ....
>
> ....
>
> ....
>
> ....

ⓑ Now underline Ⓐ the **point**, the **evidence** and the **explanation** in your paragraphs.

③ Look at your evidence. Have you stuck to facts and statistics? Using a personal experience can add interest. Rewrite ✍ **one** of your paragraphs, using a personal experience instead of facts.

....

....

....

....

....

3 How do I structure my paragraphs to create impact?

For creative writing, you should structure your paragraphs to create impact. You can do this by:

- building up to a moment of tension, action or drama
- using a one-sentence paragraph to create suspense.

1 In a creative text, you can structure a paragraph to build up to a moment of tension or drama. Number 🖉 these sentences in order to create a structure that would produce tension.

	He froze.

	Ben's heart banged in his chest as he heard a sudden knocking at the door.

	Standing in front of him was a man who was supposed to be dead.

	His palms were sweaty and his breathing came in gasps.

	Slowly he opened the door and peered out.

2 A paragraph can consist of just one sentence. Very short paragraphs can create impact by emphasising a point or creating suspense. Look again at the sentences above. Which sentence could be separated from the rest to create a short paragraph for extra impact? Write 🖉 **one** sentence explaining your choice.

....

....

3 Now look at this variation on the paragraph you read on page 51.

> It had been a long and tiring day. All Ben could think about was his aching back, his sore feet and his frozen hands. The doorbell rang just as Ben sat down. Slowly getting to his feet, Ben shuffled towards the door. He opened it wide and looked out into the dark night. On the doorstep was a large black box.

a Restructure 🖉 the paragraph above to create more impact.

....

....

....

....

....

....

....

b Can you add still more impact by adding 🖉 a one-sentence paragraph?

....

....

....

Sample response

To write paragraphs that create impact you need to think about:

- using a new paragraph for each new idea
- using topic sentences and a P.E.E. structure to make the meaning of your paragraphs clear when writing to express a point of view
- structuring your creative paragraphs to increase drama or create tension
- using one-sentence paragraphs to emphasise points or create suspense.

Now look at this exam-style writing task, which you saw at the beginning of the unit.

Exam-style question

Your local library is asking people to contribute creative writing for its website.

Write a story about an unexpected visitor. (40 marks)

> I was tucked up in bed when the doorbell rang. It was late and we were not expecting any visitors. Doors banged, keys rattled and footsteps sounded as my dad let the visitor in. Listening carefully, I could hear muffled voices coming from the hall.
>
> Getting out of bed, I crept to the top of the stairs. I still couldn't make out exactly what was being said but it sounded bad. Rusty, our German Shepherd, started barking and scratching at the kitchen door. Suddenly, I heard a crash and a cry.
>
> I didn't see my dad again for another five days.

① Read the sample answer carefully. Try reading it aloud so that you can hear the impact of the sentences and paragraphs. Then annotate 🖉 the answer, commenting on its effectiveness.

  a Comment on the use of three paragraphs. Why start a new paragraph when the narrator gets out of bed?

  b Comment on the order of the sentences within the paragraphs. How is tension built up?

  c Comment on the use of the single-sentence paragraph at the end. How does this create suspense?

Your turn!

Choose **one** of the two exam-style tasks you saw at the beginning of this unit.

Paper 1

Exam-style question

Your local library is asking people to contribute creative writing for its website.

Write a story about an unexpected visitor. **(40 marks)**

Paper 2

Exam-style question

'Teenagers are far too unfit these days. The only answer is to make them do one hour of physical education every day at school.'

Write an article for a broadsheet newspaper in which you explain your point of view on this statement. **(40 marks)**

You are going to plan and write the first three paragraphs of your response.
You should focus on writing paragraphs that create impact.

(1) Use this space to note down 🖉 some ideas.

(2) Choose ✓ the ideas that you will focus on in your three paragraphs.
Make sure you have added 🖉 detail to your ideas.

(3) Now use paper to write 🖉 **three** paragraphs, thinking carefully about:

- when to start a new paragraph
- how you open your paragraphs
- how you structure your paragraphs
- using a one-sentence paragraph to create impact.

Review your skills

Check up

Review your response to the exam-style question on page 55. Tick ✓ the column to show how well you think you have done each of the following.

	Not quite ✓	Nearly there ✓	Got it! ✓
started paragraphs	☐	☐	☐
structured my sentences to make my meaning clear	☐	☐	☐
structured my paragraphs to create impact	☐	☐	☐

Look over all of your work in this unit. Note down 🖉 **three** things you can do to improve the impact of your paragraphs.

1. ....

2. ....

3. ....

Need more practice?

You could either:

• add a paragraph to your response to the task you chose on page 55

or:

• tackle the other writing task on page 55.

How confident do you feel about each of these **skills?** Colour 🖉 in the bars.

1 How do I start paragraphs?

2 How do I structure my paragraphs to make my meaning clear?

3 How do I structure my paragraphs to create impact?

(8) Creating impact with vocabulary – writing to present a viewpoint

This unit will help you select vocabulary that adds impact when you are writing to present a viewpoint. The skills you will build are to:

- select the most effective words to avoid repetition and create impact
- use linking words and phrases to guide readers through your ideas
- use techniques that add impact to your writing.

In the exam, you will be asked to tackle writing tasks such as the one below. This unit will prepare you to write your own response to this question.

Exam-style question

'Experimenting on animals is never acceptable. If humans need medicines badly, they should test them on each other.'

Write an article for a national newspaper in which you give your views on this statement.

(40 marks)

The three key questions in the **skills boosts** will help you to create impact by selecting the most effective vocabulary.

① How do I choose the best words?

② How do I link my ideas?

③ How do I use techniques to add impact?

Look at the extract on page 58 from one student's answer to the task above.

Exam-style question

'Experimenting on animals is never acceptable. If humans need medicines badly, they should test them on each other.'

Write an article for a national newspaper in which you give your views on this statement.

(40 marks)

> A lot of small <u>animals</u> like mice, rats and rabbits are being kept in bad conditions in small cages. The <u>animals</u> just sit in there, waiting for the next experiment to start. The small cages give the <u>animals</u> no room to move around. This causes stress that causes the <u>animals</u> to behave strangely and pull out their hair or bite their nails. When someone walks past the <u>animals'</u> small cages the <u>animals</u> jump because they have learned to be frightened of humans. Do you want to be one of the humans that does this?

(1) The word <u>animal</u> has been used too often. Which of the following could have been used in some of the sentences? Tick ✓ them.

	them		us		there
	their		they		it

(2) The student has used the phrase small cages three times. This lacks impact. Can you think of alternatives to the word 'small' that would increase the impact? Note down 🖉 your ideas.

....

(3) The student has not clearly signposted the ideas in the paragraph. Annotate 🖉 the paragraph to show where you think the linking phrases below could be used to make the paragraph more powerful.

| In particular | | Consequently | | Furthermore |

(4) The paragraph ends with a rhetorical question. How does this add impact? Explain 🖉 your thoughts.

....

....

....

....

How do I choose the best words?

Synonyms are words with similar meanings. You can use them in your writing to avoid repetition and to add impact.

1 Look at these two versions of a paragraph about experimenting on animals.

> Animals are often used to test cosmetics. For this, animals have chemicals injected into their bodies and mascara put into their eyes. We should stop animals being treated in this way by testing cosmetics on humans instead of on animals.

> Animals are often used to test cosmetics. For this, they have chemicals injected into their bodies and mascara put into their eyes. We should stop them being treated in this way by testing cosmetics on humans instead.

a Underline Ⓐ the changes between the two versions.

b Which version is the most effective? Write 🖉 **one** sentence explaining your choice.

....

....

2 Synonyms can also be used to add impact to your writing.

☐	Animal testing is bad.
☐	Animal testing is brutal.
☐	Animal testing is horrific.
☐	Animal testing is barbaric.
☐	Animal testing is cruel.

a Which of these sentences would have the most impact on a reader? Number 🖉 the above sentences 1–5, with 5 being the greatest impact.

b Now come up with 🖉 some synonyms for the highlighted words in this sentence.

> Helpless animals are kept in small cages.

helpless ....

animals ....

kept...,...

cages...

2 How do I link my ideas?

To guide your reader through your ideas you should use a range of linking words and phrases. These are called **adverbials**.

(1) Copy 🖉 the adverbials below into the correct box in the table, according to their purpose.

in addition	for instance	in contrast	additionally	in particular
as a result	furthermore	significantly	in conclusion	because
likewise	therefore	secondly	especially	
however	on the other hand	next	firstly	

Adding an idea:	Explaining an idea:	Introducing an example:
Comparing or contrasting ideas:	**Emphasising important ideas:**	**Ordering ideas:**

(2) Look at these paragraphs of a student's response to the exam-style question about experiments on animals.

...., some people say that an animal's life is not as important as that of a

human. ...., it is often said that they only exist so that humans can use

them for food. ...., I believe that we should learn to love and look after all

small creatures. ...., even rats make excellent pets as they are loyal and

loving towards their owners.

...., the animals used for testing are kept in appalling conditions.

...., they are kept alone in tiny cages for most of the day with no light.

They are taken out only when they are needed for experiments, all of which are very cruel.

...., they are even kept short of water and fed only enough to keep them

alive. ...., many start to pull out their own feathers or fur.

Fill in 🖉 the gaps by using appropriate adverbial words or phrases from the boxes above.

3 How do I use techniques to add impact?

Language techniques can be used to add power and impact to your writing.

1 Look at the examples of students' writing on the left. Draw lines to match them to the correct techniques on the right.

A. | Why should innocent creatures be tortured?

B. | All kinds of animals are used including dogs, rabbits, guinea pigs and hamsters.

C. | The animals that are used are just like your beloved cat or dog.

D. | Keeping small animals alone in cages is cruel. Keeping them without food and water is cruel. Pouring chemicals into their eyes is cruel.

list

rhetorical question

repetition

direct address

2 Now use each of the techniques above to write your own sentences in response to the task on page 57 about experiments on animals.

list ....

....

....

rhetorical question ....

....

....

repetition...

....

....

direct address ....

....

....

Sample response

As you select vocabulary when writing to present a viewpoint, you need to think about creating impact by:

- using synonyms to avoid repetition
- using adverbials to guide readers through your ideas
- using language techniques to add impact.

Now look at this exam-style question again.

Exam-style question

'Experimenting on animals is never acceptable. If humans need medicines badly, they should test them on each other.'

Write an article for a national newspaper in which you give your views on this statement.

(40 marks)

Now look at this extract from one student's response to the task.

> Additionally, many of the animals that are killed by experiments are creatures that many people keep as pets. For example, dogs, cats, rabbits and guinea pigs are all hurt so that we can have medicines. In particular, experiments are done on puppies almost as soon as they are born. These puppies are kept in tiny cages. These puppies are kept without food and water for days. These puppies are then cut open before having chemicals put onto them. How would you feel if this were your animal?

(1) Read the student's paragraph aloud. How effective are the vocabulary choices this student has made?

   a Underline (A) any adverbials used to signpost you through the writing. Select **one** adverbial and explain how it helps to add impact to the writing.

   ....

   ....

   b Replace (✏) the highlighted words with words or phrases that have more impact.

   c Explain (✏) how the following add impact to the writing:

   i. A list of small animal types ....

   ....

   ii. Repetition of the word 'puppy' ....

   ....

   iii. Ending with a rhetorical question ....

   ....

Your turn!

You are now going to write three paragraphs of a response to this exam-style task.

Exam-style question

'Experimenting on animals is never acceptable. If humans need medicines badly, they should test them on each other.'

Write an article for a national newspaper in which you give your views on this statement.

(40 marks)

1 Think about all the different ideas you could include in your response.
Use the space to note down 🖊 some ideas.

2 Choose ✓ the ideas that you will focus on in your three paragraphs.
Make sure you have added 🖊 detail to your ideas.

3 Now write 🖊 your response on paper. Remember to focus on:

- using synonyms to avoid repetition and add impact
- using adverbials to guide the reader through your ideas
- using language techniques to add impact.

Review your skills

Check up

Review your response to the exam-style question on page 63. Tick ✓ the column to show how well you think you have done each of the following.

	Not quite ✓	Nearly there ✓	Got it! ✓
chosen the best words	☐	☐	☐
linked my ideas	☐	☐	☐
used techniques to add impact	☐	☐	☐

Look over all of your work in this unit. Note down 🖊 **three** ways you can add impact through your vocabulary choices:

1. ....

2. ....

3. ....

Need more practice?

Try tackling the Paper 2 question below.

Exam-style question

'Modern teenagers are lazy and spoilt. They should all be made to go out and get a part-time job.'

Write an article for a magazine in which you explain your views on this statement.   **(40 marks)**

How confident do you feel about each of these **skills?** Colour 🖊 in the bars.

1 How do I choose the best words?

2 How do I link my ideas?

3 How do I use techniques to add impact?

⑨ Creating impact with vocabulary – narrative and descriptive writing

This unit will help you select vocabulary that adds impact to your narrative and descriptive writing. The skills you will build are to:

- select words for effect
- use language techniques to create images in your readers' minds
- use the senses to develop your descriptions.

In the exam, you will be asked to tackle writing tasks such as the ones below. This unit will prepare you to write your own response to this question.

Exam-style question

You are going to enter a creative writing competition. Your entry will be judged by a panel of people of your own age.

Either: Write a description suggested by this picture.

Or: Write a story about a day trip.

(40 marks)

The three key tasks in the **skills boosts** will help you to select vocabulary for impact and effect in your narrative and descriptive writing.

1 How do I choose words for effect?

2 How do I use language techniques to create images?

3 How do I review and improve my vocabulary choices?

Look at the extracts from two students' responses on page 66 to the first exam-style task above.

Write a description suggested by this picture.

Student A

The sea glistened like a beautiful jewel. Waves lapped gently onto the rocks. Looking up, I was blinded by the sun as it rose like a giant yellow balloon. Scratchy clumps of seaweed stuck to my feet as I strolled down to the emerald green water. I sank slowly onto the soft yellow sand. The beach was a fabulous place to have a day out.

/5

Student B

The sea looked nice and cool. I could see waves coming in to the beach. The sun was very hot. Seaweed was sticking to my feet as I walked along. I sat down on the sand. I decided that this day out was going to be good fun.

/5

(1) Look closely at both extracts. Which do you think has the most effective vocabulary choices? Give each one a mark out of 5, using the scale below.

1   Vocabulary choices have no impact.

2   Vocabulary choices have some impact.

3   Vocabulary choices create a picture.

4   Vocabulary choices create a clear picture of the beach.

5   Vocabulary choices create a brilliant picture of the beach.

(2) Which of the two student extracts is the most effective? Write **one** sentence explaining your choice.

....

....

....

(3) Now look again at your choice of extract in question (1). Underline (A) any vocabulary that you feel is effective. Select **one** example that you have underlined and write **one** sentence explaining its effect.

....

....

....

How do I choose words for effect?

You can add impact to your writing by choosing emotive language. Emotive language is vocabulary that creates images in the minds of your readers. To do this, you can:

- use exciting synonyms for verbs
- use adjectives in your descriptions
- use adverbs to add impact to your verbs.

1 Look at the sentence below from one student's description of a beach.

> I saw seagulls *flying* down on to the sand as I *walked* along the beach.

Now look at some more exciting synonyms for the verbs in the sentence.

glimpsed	swooping	strolled
watched	soaring	ambled
spied	gliding	strode

....

....

a Add 🖉 one or two more synonyms to each of the columns.

b Practise using alternative verbs in place of those highlighted to add impact to the sentence. Write 🖉 out your sentences.

i. ....

ii. ....

iii. ....

2 Another way to add impact is to use **adjectives** to describe your nouns and **adverbs** to describe your verbs. For example:

> I saw *giant* seagulls flying down on to the *golden* sand as I walked *slowly* along the *deserted* beach.

a Choose the best of your sentences from question **1 b** above and add 🖉 adjectives to your nouns and adverbs to one of the verbs.

i. ....

....

ii. ....

....

iii. ....

....

b Which of your sentences is the most effective? Tick ✓ your choice. Write a sentence to explain why it is effective.

....

....

....

2 How do I use language techniques to create images?

You can add impact to your narrative and descriptive writing by using language techniques such as similes, metaphors and personification. These techniques will create powerful images in the minds of your readers.

(1) Look at these examples of sentences that use language techniques.

A. The sea was like a glistening jewel.	Personification
B. The beach was a scorching furnace by midday.	Simile
C. The waves crept closer and closer to my feet.	Metaphor

(a) Draw lines linking the sentences with the correct techniques.

(b) Choose one of the examples above and explain what image it would create in a reader's mind.

....

....

....

....

(2) Now use the techniques above to complete these sentences.

Similes:

i. The sand looked like ....

....

ii. The seagulls swooped down like a ....

....

Metaphors:

i. The beach was ....

....

ii. The ice cream was ....

....

Personification (add verbs):

i. The wind .... against my face.

ii. Seaweed .... to my feet.

(3) Write a short description of the beach using two of your ideas from question (2).

....

....

....

....

....

3 How do I review and improve my vocabulary choices?

When you have finished your narrative and descriptive writing, you should always review your vocabulary choices.

1) First, look at your writing to see if it lacks impact. For instance, this student has made some boring vocabulary choices.

> We sat very close together on the warm bus. The sun in my eyes made me feel faint. I could smell my friend's crisps and hear him chewing loudly. Out of the window I could see green fields and lots of trees.

a Which words could be improved by substituting a more exciting synonym? Underline (A) them and note down (✏) alternatives for **two** of these words.

....

....

b Draw (✏) arrows where you could add adjectives and adverbs to the student's writing. Annotate the writing with **two** more adjectives and **one** adverb.

c Where could impact be added by using a language technique? Think of a simile, metaphor or an example of personification that would improve the writing and write (✏) it below.

....

....

2) Second, review your vocabulary to see if you have chosen words or phrases that are not very original. For instance, this student uses phrases that are so overused that they lack impact.

> Stella burst into floods of tears. She was normally as brave as a lion but something had really spooked her this time. I could see she was already frightened to death as she was white as a sheet.

a Underline (A) any words or phrases that you think are not very original.

b Select **one** and replace (✏) it with vocabulary or a language technique that is original enough to create impact.

....

....

....

c Now rewrite (✏) the paragraph, replacing the words and phrases you underlined in a with vocabulary that creates impact.

....

....

....

Unit 9 Creating impact with vocabulary – narrative and descriptive writing   69

Sample response

When you select vocabulary for your narrative and descriptive writing, you should think about:

- using exciting synonyms for verbs
- adding adjectives and adverbs to your nouns and verbs
- using similes, metaphors or personification to create powerful images
- reviewing all your vocabulary choices to make sure they are original and exciting.

Now look at one student's response to the beach picture you saw on page 65.

I stared up at the shops and cafés that lined the beach. A cool summer breeze wafted over my face. As I strolled slowly along the fine golden sand the delicious smell of hotdogs floated towards me. Seagulls swooped onto the beach like vultures, pouncing on empty crisps packets and sandwich crusts.

People trudged past me like an army going to war. When they reached the beach they set out their towels like carpets as their children rushed about clutching bright red buckets and spades. The waves lapped at their feet as they danced about in the water.

---

1. Underline (A) and label (✏) any examples of simile, metaphor and personification.
2. Circle (A) **five** vocabulary choices that you feel add impact to the writing.
3. Choose **two** of the choices you have circled and explain (✏) the effect of the vocabulary.

....

....

4. For each of the highlighted words or phrases, think of **two** alternatives, then tick (✓) the ones you feel are most effective:

strolled slowly	.... ☐	.... ☐
fine golden	.... ☐	.... ☐
trudged	.... ☐	.... ☐
bright red	.... ☐	.... ☐
danced	.... ☐	.... ☐

Your turn!

You are now going to write your response to one of these exam-style tasks.

Exam-style question

You are going to enter a creative writing competition. Your entry will be judged by a panel of people of your own age.

Either: Write a description suggested by this picture.

Or: Write a story about a day trip.

(40 marks)

1) Think about all the different ideas you might include in your response. Use this space to note them down.

2) Choose the ideas that you will focus on. Number them to show the structure you will use. Make sure you have added detail to each of your ideas.

3) Now write your response on paper. Remember to focus on:

- using emotive language
- using language techniques to add impact.

4) When you have finished writing, go back and review all your vocabulary choices. Amend any you think could be improved.

Review your skills

Check up

Review your response to the exam-style task on page 71. Tick ✓ the column to show how well you think you have done each of the following.

	Not quite ✓	Nearly there ✓	Got it! ✓
chosen words for effect	☐	☐	☐
used language techniques to create images	☐	☐	☐
reviewed and improved my vocabulary choices	☐	☐	☐

Look over all of your work in this unit. Note down ✐ **three** ways you can add impact through your vocabulary choices:

1. ....

2. ....

3. ....

Need more practice?

Tackle the other writing task from page 71. Remember to focus closely on selecting, reviewing and improving your vocabulary choices.

How confident do you feel about each of these **skills?** Colour ✐ in the bars.

1 How do I choose words for effect?

2 How do I use language techniques to create images?

3 How do I review and improve my vocabulary choices?

Answers

Unit 1

Page 2

(1) **Plan C**: too many events mean nothing will be developed with interesting details

Plan B: no real ending to story

Plan A: story is dull and a bit predictable: no excitement for reader

Page 5

(1) For example:

Beginning: All my friends were jealous; Went out with friends on bike and beat them all.

Middle: Have big breakfast and drive to race.

(3) **a** For example: Narrator could be hero as he could save best friend rather than winning.

b For example: Best friend could be villain as he could crash into narrator deliberately.

Unit 2

Page 10

(1) A

(2) **a** For example: Many people neglect friends and family as they spend too long online.

Page 11

(1) 'The internet, far from being the greatest invention of the 20th century, is a dangerous and extremely harmful tool.'

Write the text for a speech in which you explain your point of view on this statement.

For example: format – speech; writing – formal; purpose – to inform/explain a point of view; audience – need facts and opinions about the internet.

Page 13

(1) **a** A or C

b B

Page 14

(1) **a** 'Difficult to use' and 'Some areas don't have wifi' should be crossed out as they do not support the chosen point of view.

b Points could be joined as follows:

Online shopping – Get stuff delivered

Educational games – Many useful apps are free – Games with friends

Find old friends – Communicate for free – Keep in touch

Get information easily – Watch TV anywhere

Unit 3

Page 19

(1) **a** Create a mystery – I know I shouldn't have told the lie...; Start with conflict – I froze...; Start with action – Crash!...

Page 20

(1) A

Unit 4

Page 27

(1) **a** Points 1 and 4 are arguably the strongest.

Page 28

(1) **a** Rhetorical question

b Fact/statistic or Strong statement

(3) A

Page 29

(1) **a** question

b warning

Page 30

(1) and **(2)** For example: The introduction is dull and does not add enough detail to support the view of the writer. A technique such as a rhetorical question could be used, or a strong statistic to shock the audience.

Unit 5

Page 34

(1) **a** Both sentences are too long.

b Too many commas have been used instead of starting a new sentence.

(2) For example:

a Proper noun 'Barry' needs capital letter.

b Exclamation marks are overused.

c Apostrophe is missing from 'Barry's' and wrongly included in 'sells'.

d Sentences 4 and 5 could be joined as they are both about Barry's work in the restaurant.

Page 35

(1) For example: I loved my job in the **city.** I worked in a large fashion store and loved meeting lots of different people. I should never have moved to the country **as** I had to leave all my friends behind. The countryside was very green and peaceful **but** it was sometimes too quiet.

(2) For example: I only found out they were bulls when one charged at me!

(3) For example: I always want to win even if I am just playing Monopoly with my mates! Who doesn't want to win? Those who say winning doesn't matter are just losers. They probably just don't want to try hard at anything. Competition is good for you as you learn something even if you don't come first.

Page 36

(1) **(a)** For example: Taking part in competitions is good for you but not everybody thinks winning is important.

(b) For example: We all need to learn what it is like to lose if we want to appreciate the joy of winning.

Page 37

(1) **(a)** For example: The weather was cold, blustery and very wet.

(b) For example: We all need to learn how to play fairly, how to lose gracefully and how to enjoy the game.

(2) **(a)** For example: My friend, who is very good at football, told me I was making a big mistake.

(b) For example: It was at the park, where I play netball every weekend, that I made my first mistake.

(c) For example: My first football trophy, which is silver-plated, stands on the mantelpiece.

Page 38

For example:

My big mistake was telling everything to my friend Alice. Alice, the girl who lived next door, was the perfect friend and we did everything together. I thought she was the kindest, funniest person I had ever met. As we grew up, we shared clothes, make-up and even our deepest secrets about everything. When I met John, who was my brother's friend, at tennis lessons, I told Alice how much I liked him. I knew she would want to meet him. I didn't think that she would want him for herself!

Unit 6

Page 42

(1) A and B

(2) C

Page 43

(1) Sentences should use a variety of different openings.

Page 44

(1) For example: If we all stopped donating to charity, the government would have to do more about poverty.

(2) For example: I took my eyes off the road and turned to stare at her when I finally realised what she was telling me.

Page 46

For example:

(1) **(a)** There is some variety as the student has used an -ing verb, a preposition, an article and pronouns. This makes the paragraph more exciting to read.

(b) The sentence structures are varied.

(c) The final short sentence makes the reader want to know if anybody is hurt in the crash and what happens next. An alternative could be: 'I don't remember what happened next.'

Unit 7

Page 50

(2) Mark new paragraph before 'Most teenagers do not take the recommended amount of exercise

(3) **(a)** teenagers spend lots of time in front of a computer screen

(b) most teenagers do not get enough exercise

(4) Many teenagers, particularly boys, spend hours in front of computer games.

Girls spend hours on the internet.

I see young people catch the bus to school even if they live close enough to walk.

Page 51

(1) For example: Teenagers do not take enough daily exercise.

(2) For example:

i. Later, Ben remembered that day as the last time he was happy.

ii. Tom shut the back door firmly and walked into the lounge.

Page 52

(1) **Point:** Teenage obesity is a big problem in the UK. **Evidence:** A recent survey showed that eighty-five percent of teenagers do not take the recommended daily amount of exercise. Instead of playing sports outside, they are spending all their time in front of a computer screen. **Explanation:** This inactivity will make the obesity situation a lot worse if we do nothing.

(2) **a/b** For example: **Point:** Daily exercise has many benefits. **Evidence:** For example, it helps boost blood to your brain cells. **Explanation:** This means that even a short walk to school can help you get better grades in your GCSEs.

(3) For example: Daily exercise has many benefits. I played football every lunchtime at school for the whole of Year 11. By the end of the year, I felt much fitter and had lost over a stone in weight.

Page 53

(1) For example:

5 He froze.

1 Ben's heart banged in his chest as he heard a sudden knocking at the door.

4 Standing in front of him was a man who was supposed to be dead.

2 His palms were sweaty and his breathing came in gasps.

3 Slowly he opened the door and peered out.

(2) He froze.

(3) **a** For example: The doorbell rang just as Ben sat down. It had been a long and tiring day. All Ben could think about was his aching back, his sore feet and his frozen hands. Slowly getting to his feet, Ben shuffled towards the door. He opened it wide and looked out into the dark night. On the doorstep was a large black box.

   b It was ticking.

Page 54

(1) For example:

   a A new paragraph is needed because the action moves to the hall.

   b The tense part is delayed until the end of the paragraph.

   c The reader will want to know what happens in those five days.

Unit 8

Page 58

(1) them, their, they

(2) tiny, under-sized, inadequate

(3) For example: Consequently, the animals just sit in there...

   Furthermore, when someone walks past...

(4) The rhetorical question adds impact by suddenly shifting the focus from the animals' plight to the humans who cause it, demanding that the reader take some blame for the situation.

Page 59

(1) **b** Version 2 is the more effective as it does not repeat the word 'animals'.

Page 60

(1)

Adding an idea:	Explaining an idea:	Introducing an example:
in addition	as a result	for instance
additionally	because	
furthermore	therefore	
Comparing or contrasting ideas:	Emphasising important ideas:	Ordering ideas:
likewise	significantly	secondly
however	especially	next
on the other hand	in particular	firstly
in contrast		in conclusion

(2) **a** For example – second paragraph:

   <u>Firstly</u>, the animals used for testing are kept in appalling conditions. <u>For instance</u>, they are kept alone in tiny cages for most of the day with no light. They are taken out only when they are needed for experiments, all of which are very cruel. <u>Additionally</u>, they are even kept short of water and fed only enough to keep them alive. <u>As a result</u>, many start to pull out their own feathers or fur.

Page 61

(1) A – rhetorical question; B – list; C – direct address; D – repetition

Unit 9

Page 66

(1) **(2)** and **(3)** Student A's response contains effective descriptive vocabulary such as 'glistened', 'beautiful', 'lapped', 'scratchy', 'emerald', etc.

Page 68

(1) **a** A simile; B metaphor; C personification

Published by Pearson Education Limited, 80 Strand, London, WC2R ORL.

www.pearsonschoolsandfecolleges.co.uk

Text © Pearson Education Limited 2017
Produced and typeset by Tech-Set Ltd, Gateshead

The right of Julie Hughes to be identified as author of this work has been asserted by her in accordance with the Copyright, Designs and Patents Act 1988.

First published 2017

20 19 18 17
10 9 8 7 6 5 4 3 2 1

British Library Cataloguing in Publication Data
A catalogue record for this book is available from the British Library

ISBN 978 0435 18322 6

Printed in Slovakia by Neografia

Picture Credits
The publisher would like to thank the following for their kind permission to reproduce their photographs:

(Key: b-bottom; c-centre; l-left; r-right; t-top)

Imagestate Media: John Foxx Collection 17, 21; **Pearson Education Ltd:** Gareth Boden 1, 3, 7; **Shutterstock.com:** Christian Mueller 24, Dan Breckwoldt 65, 66, 71, Ollyy 8

All other images © Pearson Education